Beyond the flavour

A story of love, memories and delicious meals

MAPLE
PUBLISHERS

Beyond The Flavour

Author: HTB Community Café Team

Copyright © 2024 HTB Community Café Team

The right of HTB Community Café Team to be identified as author of this work has been asserted by the author in accordance with section 77 and 78 of the Copyright, Designs and Patents Act 1988.

First Published in 2024

ISBN 978-1-83538-272-1 (Paperback)
     978-1-83538-271-4 (Hardback)

Foreword, Acknowledgements and Blurb by Clay Amira

Illustrations and Design by Ulrike Mieke Marais

Published by:

    Maple Publishers

    Fairbourne Drive, Atterbury,

    Milton Keynes,

    MK10 9RG, UK

    www.maplepublishers.com

"Let's build longer tables, not higher fences."

Foreword

Dear Readers,

Welcome to "Beyond the flavour" where every recipe tells a story of love, and every dish carries a special memory. In this book, we embark on a global journey that celebrates unity and diversity. We bring exotic flavours into your home. These recipes are designed by our friends who are displaced people - refugees and asylum seekers - from El Salvador, Iran, Tunisia, Lebanon, and Sudan. We have spent the last two years together as one big community and compiled our delicious dishes. We are glad to be able to share them with you.

In this book you will find a range of exciting dishes from cherished family recipes passed down through generations of Persian culture, to the rhythmic melodies that inspire the Latin American tradition. From the rich and flavourful North African cuisines, influenced by Mediterranean, Berber, Ottoman and Arabic cultures. To the aromatic Middle Eastern cuisine and the delectable East African flavours.

Whether you are a seasoned chef or a novice in the kitchen, there is something for everyone in these pages. Explore the vibrant flavours of international cuisine, discover the simplicity of one-pot wonders, and indulge in decadent desserts that will satisfy any sweet tooth.

More than just a collection of recipes, each recipe tells a story of a fond and cherished memory. Our hope is that this memory will bring joy to your table, moments of laughter, lively conversations, and the love that nourishes both body and soul.

Are you ready? Grab your apron and join us on this culinary adventure around the world. May these recipes bring warmth to your home and joy to your kitchen.

Happy cooking!

Warm regards,
Clay Amira

Middle East. pg10

North Africa. pg20

Latin America pg.32

East Africa pg.42

Acknowledgements pg.51

Middle East

Adas polo, ba gosht

Lentil rice with minced lamb

Serves 4

This is a traditional food from Iran. We serve it for celebrations, parties, gatherings with friends and families, and even funerals. Persian cuisine varies from the south to the north, and from the east to the west of Iran. Each region has different traditional foods, but this dish is made all over Iran.

350 g Rice
50 g Lentils
200 g Oil
300 g Mince lamb
3 Onions
1 tsp Turmeric
1 tsp Cinnamon
½ tsp Saffron
½ cup Raisins
Salt & Black pepper, to taste

Yoghurt salad
¼ Cabbage, thinly sliced
Tomatoes, sliced into
half moons
1 Cucumber, sliced into
half moons
1 Carrot, grated
Salt & Black pepper, to taste
Mayonnaise
Juice from 1 lemon

Prepare the rice and lentils
Wash the rice and then add it to a bowl. Soak the rice in cold water and set aside for 1 hour. Add water to a pot over medium-high heat, once boiling add the rice and salt. Once the rice is half cooked - it should be firm in the center and soft on the outside, drain and rinse with cold water, set aside for later.

Wash the lentils and cook in a pot of water over medium-high heat. Once cooked, drain and set aside. To a large pot, place a layer of rice into the pot, place a layer of cooked lentils, then another layer of rice, continue building it into a pyramid shape. Cover with a lid and cook on medium-low and steam for 1 hour.

Prepare the fried raisins
While the rice is steaming, heat 1 tbsp of oil in a saucepan over medium heat. Add the onions and washed raisins, and sauté for about 5-minutes. Then add turmeric and cinnamon and fry again a little until combined. Remove the raisins and onion to a plate. Prepare the saffron: To a small bowl, add the saffron with 2 tbsp hot water to dissolve.

"Cooking this dish makes me very happy, as I used to cook it with my family in Iran. Persian cuisine varies with different regions in Iran, but Adas Polo is eaten in all parts of the country, so I hope that this dish reminds Iranians of home."
— Nastaran, Iran

Cook the meat
Slice the onions and fry in a saucepan until lightly browned, then add the minced meat and fry until it is well cooked. Then add a small spoonful of turmeric, cinnamon, black pepper and a pinch of salt and fry for a minute. Finally, add the saffron to the ingredients.

Serving
Once the rice is ready, lightly mix the layers of lentils and rice together to combine. Serve the rice on a plate and garnish with the sauteed raisin and the minced lamb.

This dish goes well with a yoghurt salad: Slice cabbage, tomatoes and cucumbers, and grate the carrots. Mix all the salad ingredients together and add lemon juice with a little salt, black pepper to taste and mayonnaise.

Zereshk polo

Barberry rice and saffron chicken

Serves 4

400 g Rice
4 Chicken Legs
2 Onions
1 tube Tomato Puree
200 g Oil
100 g Barberry
½ tsp Saffron
1 tsp Turmeric
1 tsp Cinnamon
Salt & Black pepper, to taste

Prepare the chicken
Wash the chicken legs and add rub them in salt. Let them marinate for an hour. In a small bowl, add half the saffron with 2 tbsp hot water to dissolve, and rub it on the chicken. Lightly brown both sides of the chicken and set aside. Slice the onions and fry in a saucepan until lightly browned. Add the tomato paste, turmeric, cinnamon and black pepper and let it cook for 5 minutes. Then add 3 cups of water. Place the chicken into the sauce mixture and simmer for 45 minutes.

Prepare the rice
Wash the rice and then add it to a bowl. Soak the rice in cold water and set aside for 2 hours. Add the soaked rice to a pot of boiling salted water, and cook for 15 minutes. Drain the rice in a colander. Heat some oil in a large pot, add the cooked rice to cover the base, and let it cook for an hour.

Prepare the barberry
Wash the barberry. Heat two tsp of oil in a pan, add the barberry with one tsp of sugar, and fry for about 5 minutes on low heat.

Prepare the saffron
To a small bowl, add half the saffron with 2 tbsp hot water to dissolve. Add 10 spoonfuls of cooked rice and stir.

Serving
Place a base layer of rice on a plate, and top which a layer of saffron rice. Scatter the barberry on top, and serve next to the chicken.

Estamboli

Rice with green beans and minced lamb

Serves 4

350 g Rice
200 g Green beans
200 g Minced lamb
1 tube Tomato puree
200 g Oil
2 Onions
1 tsp Turmeric
1 tsp Cinnamon
½ tsp Saffron
Salt & Black pepper, to taste

Prepare the rice
Wash the rice and then add to a bowl with cold water. Set aside for 2 hours to soak. Add the soaked rice to a pot of boiling salted water, and cook for 15 minutes. Drain the rice using a colander to remove excess water. Set aside

Prepare the meat
Slice the onions and fry in a saucepan with the oil until lightly browned. Add the minced meat to the pan and fry it with the onion for half an hour, stirring and breaking any clumps. Halfway through, add the turmeric, cinnamon, salt and black pepper and stir through for 1 minute. Then add the tomato puree and mix until fully combined. Cut the beans into 3cm pieces, wash, and cook in boiling water for 20 minutes or until tender. Add the beans to the meat, stir into the mixture to combine. After 10 minutes, remove from the heat. Stir in the saffron mixture and set aside.

Layering and cooking
To a pot, layer the rice and meat by adding a base layer of rice, and then the meat mixture, and repeat. Ensure each layer is evenly distributed. Place the pot over low heat and cook for 1 and a half hours covered to trap steam. Then serve to a plate or bowl and enjoy!

Adasi

Persian Lentil Stew

Serves 6 to 8

400 g Green Lentils
2-3 tbsp Oil
2 Medium Onions, sliced
2 Large Potatoes, cubed
1 tube Tomato puree
1 tsp Turmeric
1 tsp Neem

Soak the lentils in water for one hour, then drainn, ensure they are well-rinsed.

Slice the onions and fry in a saucepan with oil until lightly browned.
Add the lentils, tomato puree, neem and turmeric to the onions and fry for 2 minutes so the flavours develop.

Cube your potatoes and add to the lentil mixture, stir until evenly distributed.

Pour enough water to cover and simmer for an hour, or until the lentils are tender. Stir occasionally to prevent sticking and for even cooking.

Once the lentils are cooked, ladle the stew into bowls and serve hot.

Halim

Persian meat porridge

Serves 4

400 g Wheat flakes (pearl
wheat), washed and soaked
for at least 4 hours
400 g Lamb shoulder,
boneless
1 Onion, quartered
1-2 tsp Cinnamon or to taste
100 g Sugar
100g Oil
Salt to taste

Prepare the porridge
Wash the wheat rinse well. Soak it in water for at minimum of
4 hours. Pour the wheat into a deep pan of water (7 times the
weight of the wheat or). Cook on low heat for 2-3 hours until the
wheat is cooked through and has a porridge-like consistency or
as per package instructions.

Prepare the meat
Place the meat in a pot with the quartered onions. Season with
salt and add enough water to cover by 2 inches. Cover and
cook on medium heat for 1-1.5 hours or until the meat is tender.
Remove the meat from the pot and shred. Set aside.

Prepare and serve the dish
Combine the meat and cooked wheat in a potand blend
together with an immersion blender until smooth. Be careful not
to overblend, there should still be some texture from the shredded
meat.
To a small bowl, combine the sugar and cinnamon.

Ladle into bowls and top with the sugar and cinnamon mixture.

North Africa

Maekaruna Lahma Batatan

Pasta with minced lamb and potato salad

Serves 5 to 6

Pasta

500 g Pasta
200 ml Oil
400 g Minced lamb
4 Garlic cloves
1 tsp Turmeric
1 tsp Paprika
1 tube of Tomato puree (150g)
Salt & Pepper, to taste

Potato salad

4 Medium Potatoes, cut into
2 cm chunks
115 g Mayonnaise (¼ cup)
60 g Plain yoghurt (¼ cup)
1 tbsp Olive Oil
½ Lemon, juiced

Pasta

Prepare the meat sauce: In a large pan on medium heat, combine the oil, minced garlic, turmeric, paprika, tomato paste and salt & pepper. Stir gently and simmer for 30 minutes.

Add the minced lamb to the pan, break up the meat into smaller chunks using a wooden spoon. Cook for a further 30 minutes until cooked through.

Whilst the meat is cooking, cook the pasta – add the pasta to a pot of salted boiling water and cook according to package instructions. To serve: spoon the pasta into bowls and top with the meat sauce

Potato salad

Peel the potatoes, and cut into 2 cm chunks. Place potato chunks in salted boiling water and cook until tender for roughly 25 minutes.

Drain the potatoes in a colander. Combine the potato with equal parts mayonnaise and plain yoghurt, 1 tbsp of olive oil and the juice of half a lemon.

Serve on a small side plate next to the pasta

"I learnt my cooking from my mother, who taught me every step of the way. I enjoy coming to the community cafe and seeing others enjoy what I cook."
— Kheira, Tunisia

Tip: Cook your pasta with a few bay leaves, it gives a lovely flavour — Kheira

Maekaruna Lahma Batatan Pasta with minced lamb and potato salad, page 22-23

Dajaj foutour arz

Chicken and mushrooms with Rice

Serves 4 to 5

57 g Butter
1.5 kg Chicken, use any cut
1 kg Mushrooms, we use small button cut in half
2 Medium Carrots, cut into 2cm chunks
1 Cauliflower, cut into florets
300 ml Cream
Splash of milk
350 g Basmati rice

Cook the rice
Wash the rice, I like to wash the rice four times. Cook the rice as per package instructions, or as follows: To a pot add hot water and a pinch of salt. Add the rice and cook over medium heat for 20 minutes. Then drain the rice and steam in the pot for 20 minutes.

Cook the chicken
To a pot, heat the butter over medium heat.

Once melted, add the chicken with a pinch of salt & pepper. Fry until the sides of the chicken are golden and cooked through. Then add the mushrooms, carrots and cauliflower and stir until cooked.

Finally, add the cream and a splash of milk and stir until well combined.

Serve the chicken over the cooked basmati rice.

Arz Lahma

Rice with lamb and nuts

Serves 10 to 12

1 kg rice
1 kg lamb shoulder, diced into
4cm pieces
½ tbsp Turmeric
300g + 2 tbsp butter
1 sprig Rosemary
Salt and pepper, to taste
Rosemary
500 g Almonds, whole

Prepare the rice
Rinse the rice and place into a pot of boiling water with 300 g
of butter. Cook on a low heat for 30 minutes until rice is cooked
through and then drain.

Cook the Lamb
Cut the lamb into 4 cm pieces. To a pot of boiling water, add the
lamb, salt, pepper, turmeric and rosemary. Simmer until meat is
cooked and tender.

Prepare the almonds
In a pan over medium heat, melt 2 tbsp of butter. Once the butter
begins to bubble, add the almonds. Stir frequently and turn off
heat and transfer to kitchen towel once they start to brown.

Serving
Spoon the rice onto a plate. Add the lamb pieces on top.
Sprinkle the buttered almonds and serve.

Couscous Lahma

Couscous with lamb and vegetables

Serves 5 to 6

2 kg Lamb, preferably Lamb
shoulder cut into pieces
1 kg Couscous
75 ml oil, olive traditionally
used but others work
3 Onions, diced
1 tsp Paprika
1 tsp Turmeric
1 tsp Cumin
500 g Tomato paste
3 Medium Carrots, peeled
and cut lengthwise in half
3 Medium Potatoes, peeled
and cut lengthwise in half
1 tin of Chickpeas, drained
½ Cabbage, cut into 2-inch
square chunks
Salt and pepper to taste

Prepare the couscous
Cook the couscous as per the package instructions. Or as
follows: To a pot, add 750ml of water and bring to a boil
medium-high heat. Once boiling, turn off the heat and add
the 1kg of couscous, stir and then cover with a lid. Cook the
couscous for roughly 10 minutes without touching it. Once done,
gently fluff the couscous with a fork and set aside.

Cook the Lamb
In a large pot over medium heat, heat the olive oil, tomato paste,
paprika, turmeric, cumin, salt, and pepper. Stir well to combine.
Add the lamb pieces to the pot and sear the sides until browned,
about 3-5 minutes.

Add the onions, carrots, potatoes, chickpeas, and cabbage to
the pot. Pour in enough boiling water to cover the vegetables,
roughly 3 glasses.

Cover the pot with a lid and simmer over medium-low heat for
about 15 minutes or until the vegetables are cooked and tender
(when a fork easily pierces the vegetable).

To serve
Add the couscous to a bowl, then add the meat and
vegetables on top.

Arz Baamia

Okra with rice

Serves 5 to 6

1 kg Rice
3 kg Okra, cut into 4cm
pieces
1 tsp Turmeric Powder
2 tbsp Paprika Powder
200 g or 1 tube Tomato paste
A handful of Coriander, roughly chopped
3 cloves Garlic
70 g Butter (5 tbsp)
400 ml oil

Prepare the rice
Add the rice to salted boiling water with the other half of the
turmeric. Cook for 20 minutes. Drain the rice and return to pan
with butter. Cook for further 15 minutes on low heat.

Prepare the Okra
In a large pan on medium high heat, simmer the oil, tomato
paste, half the turmeric, paprika, salt and pepper for 2 minutes.
Chop the okra into 4 cm pieces. Add 5 cups of boiling water to
the pan. Then add the okra and cook for 20 minutes.
Roughly chop the coriander and add to the pan for a further
10 minutes.

To serve
Spoon the buttery rice onto a plate, and top with okra.

1

Latin America

Pupusas with salsa 'Pupusa Salvadorenas

El Savadorean Flatbread with salsa

Serves 4

This is a signature El Salvadorean flatbread with salsa snack, that can be enjoyed at all times of the day. We mainly eat it at the weekends.

340 g Harina Pan (12 oz)
100 g Refried Beans
200 g Grated Firm Queso Mozzarella
400 g Tomato Paste
½ Onion
1 Chicken Stock Cube
400 ml Water

Salad:
½ Cabbage, grated or finely sliced
Oregano, to taste
Salt, to taste
1 Carrot, grated
250 ml Apple Cider Vinegar, or to taste

Prepare the dough
Dissolve the flour with 400 ml warm water, mix until smooth. Cover with a towel and set aside for later.

Prepare the filling
Chop the tomatoes, onions, green chillies into 4 cm pieces. Blend ¾ of the tomatoes, ½ onions and 3 green chilies till smooth and set aside.Fry the beans in a pan over medium heat, add salt to taste. Stir constantly until reduced and a firmer paste remains. When they're done, add the mozzarella cheese and set aside.

Prepare the salsa
In a blender, blend ¼ of the tomatoes, ¼ of the onions and 2 green chilies and chicken stock cube until smooth. Add to a pan and bring to a boil for 20 minutes or until thickened. Set aside

Prepare the salad
Grate half a cabbage, place in a bowl. Pour boiling water over it and leave for half an hour then drain. Add oregano, salt to taste, grated carrot. apple cider vinegar and Stir till combined and set aside.

"Cooking reminds me of family. I learnt to cook from my mother and cooking in a restaurant in El Salvador. Now I cook for my family and share my home comfort meals with others."
– Lilli, El Salvador

Prepare the pupusa and serve

Divide the dough into golf ball-sized portions and using your hands flatten each dough ball to make a tortilla shape or form a ¼ inch thick patty.

Place 1-2 tbsp of the filling in the center of the patty.
Close the dough by pressing with the palm of your hands, or fold the edges of the dough over the filling, then seal to form a ball again. Flatten each stuffed dough ball to form thick tortillas.
Place on a griddle, over medium heat, cook the pupusa for a few minutes on both sides until golden brown.

Serve the pupusas on a plate with the salsa in a small bowl to the side with the salad.

How to make a Pupusa

1. Take a small amount of dough to form a ball.

2. Form a ball in your hands. Size of an apple.

3. Using the palm of your hands, flatten it into a disk.

4. Make a small purse shape using your fingers.

5. Fill this with your chicken, forming a ball again.

6. Forming a bag shape, pinch off the top of extra dough.

7. Flattening it out into a disk, ready to fry it.

El Salvadorean 'Panes con Pollo Salvadoreños'

El Salvadorean Chicken Sandwich

Serves 6

Panes con Pollo Salvadoreños is a traditional Salvadoran chicken sandwich for all occasions including Christmas and Birthdays.

6 White Sandwich Rolls
1 Whole Medium Chicken
10 Large Tomatoes
3 Onions
5 Green Chilies
100 g Mustard
2 Cucumbers
2 heads of Lettuce, iceberg or romaine shredded
1 lemon
Chicken broth
Salt and Pepper to taste

Prepare the chicken

Season the chicken with salt and lemon juice, then cut in half down the middle. Rub the chicken with a mixture of mustard and chicken broth. Further cut the chicken into 6-10 pieces that are suitable for frying. In a large pan with olive oil, fry the chicken pieces until golden brown. Remove the chicken meat from the bone and finely shred using a fork or your hands.

Prepare the filling

Chop the tomatoes and onions into 4 cm pieces and finely slice the green chilies. In a blender, add the tomatoes, onions, green chilies, chicken broth and salt to taste, with 5 cups of water. Blend till a consistent texture. Transfer to a pot and bring to a boil. Then reduce heat and simmer for 20 minutes, until thickened. Add the shredded chicken meat to the sauce and mix thoroughly. Adjust seasoning if necessary.

Assemble the sandwich

Slice the tomatoes and cucumbers into 2 cm slices, and roughly shred the lettuce. Slice the bread in half without cutting all the way through and add the vegetables to coat. Place the chicken filling on top of the vegetables and close the sandwich.

Budin de guineo y pan

Bread Pudding

Serves 12

This Salvadorean bread pudding dessert with a caramel sauce is cooked in a water bath and best served at room temperature or warm. Traditional budin includes raisins, but we leave them out.

1 L Milk
8 oz bread (8 French loaves/ Pan de aguea or 12 slices of bread)
6 eggs
113 g Margarine (or 1 stick)
3 ripe bananas or 5 bananas
300 g Sugar (1 ½ cup)
1 tsp Baking Powder
1 tsp Vanilla, to taste

Bread Pudding
Mash the bread into crumbles and small pieces. In a large bowl, whisk the milk, eggs and melted butter. Then add the bread and bananas and stir till combined. Then stir 200 g (1 cup) of sugar, the baking powder and ½ tsp vanilla, mix till just combined. Set aside.

Prepare the Caramel
In a skillet add the the remaining 100g (½ cup) sugar and ½ tsp Vanilla. Gently cook over low heat, stirring constantly to dissolve the sugar and prevent from burning. Once the sugar is dissolved, stop stirring and bring to a boil over medium heat for 5-7 minutes or until an even golden colour – watch it careful. Then remove from the heat and pour into a large pudding dish and let cool.

Assemble and Serve
Preheat the oven to 200°C. Add the bread pudding mixture to the dish. Place the dish in a larger dish filled with water and bake for 1 ½ hours, or until the top is golden brown and a toothpick inserted in the center comes out clean. If the toothpick does not come out clean, continue cooking until done.
Once ready, remove from the oven and allow to cool slightly before unmolding. For best results, refrigerate for at least 2 hours or overnight to let the pudding set and develop its flavor. Before serving, bring to room temperature, then turn the dish over onto a tray and carefully unmold.

Empanadas de platano Salvadorenas'

Banana Empanadas

Serves 4

Popular treat of deep-fried plantain stuffed with a milk custard and dusted with sugar.

2 ripe Plantains
500 ml Milk
250 g Cornstarch
1 cinnamon stick
1 bottle Neutral Oil, for frying
50 g sugar, or to taste

Prepare the plantain
Wash the plantains well, remove the ends, peel and cut into 3 sections. Boil the bananas in half a liter of water. then remove, and let it site. Then smash the bananas until you get a puree.

Prepare the dough
Mix the cornstarch with the milk and a cinnamon stick.
Cook on a low heat stirring constantly until it reaches a firm consistency, then remove from the heat and let it cool completely

Prepare & cook the empanada
Split the dough into 4 balls, flatten the balls into a round flat but not thin disk. Place a spoonful of the plantain filling inside the centre of a portion of dough, and repeat to make the 10 portions. Close the balls, sealing the filling inside the dough. Place them on oiled pans or plates and gently press down each ball with a dish to make a disc. In a pan, heat oil over a medium heat.

Fry the empanadas on for 2-3 minutes until lightly fried, and then flip to cook the other side.

Drain on paper towels and then lightly dust the empanadas with sugar to serve.

East Africa

"The Sudanese kitchen has a diverse range of dishes, with every part of Sudan having its own regional specialties, although we also share some common dishes. They can be served for celebrations, parties, Eids, gatherings with friends and family, or even funerals. I learnt to cook my traditional home food from watching YouTube videos and from friends and family. I cook for my friends to provide home comfort and to enjoy our traditional home foods." – Mahmoud, Sudan

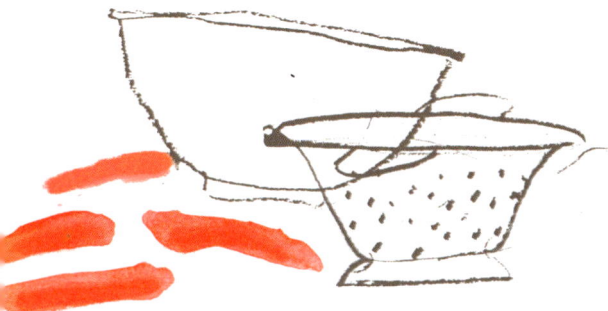

mulah Damea

Sudanese Meat Stew

Serves 4

This is a classic Sudanese meat stew dish. We eat this with Sudanese flatbread, Asida/Aseeda (page 48) and Dukwa salat (page 48).

1 kg Lamb, beef or chicken
250 g Oil
2 Onions, finely chopped
2 Green pepper, finely chopped
Salt, to taste
4 Garlic cloves, finely chopped
2-3 tbsp Tomato paste
2 medium potatoes, peeled and cut into chunks
1-2 tsp Coriander powder
Parsley

Chop the onions and garlic. Then add to a pot with 1-2 tbsp oil over low heat and stir until melted or translucent.

Add the meat, browning on all sides and then until fully cooked through.

Then add the tomato paste and stir until combined.

After 10 minutes add the peeled potato, green peppers, the spices. and the salt. Stir until fully combined.

Add water to cover all the ingredients and cook for 40 minutes on medium-high, add salt if needed.

Remove from the stove and serve with Sudanese flatbread.

mullah Robe

Minced Lamb Stew with Yoghurt 'Mullah Robe'

Serves 4 to 5

4 tbsp of Neutral Oil
4 Medium onions, finely
chopped
6 Garlic cloves
1 kg Minced Lamb
4 tbsp Peanut butter
245 g Yoghurt (1 cup)
946 ml Water (4 cups)
4 tbsp Tomato Paste
Salt, to taste

Chop the onions finely, then put them in the pot with oil and cook until brown.

Add the minced meat and cook for 5 minutes, stirring to combine and breaking the meat apart.

Then add peanut butter and tomato paste and combine, then add the yogurt and keep mixing. Add 4 cups of water and simmer for 10 minutes until it boiling.

Lower the heat and cook for 5 more minutes. Add salt to taste and cook for 5 more minutes.

Take off the heat and serve in a bowl with Sudanese bread.

Aseeda / Asida

Sudanese Wheat Porridge

Serves 4, served as a side dish

Aseeda is made by simply cooking flour into a thick porridge or dough. It is a traditional Sudanese dish, typically eaten with mullah stews.

500 ml Boiled water, or more depending on consistency
500g Sorghum or millet flour (2 cups)

Boil 500L of water and then add the flour to the pot.

Stir rapidly and cook for 5-10 minutes till no lumps, and the mixture is thick.

Allow to cool for 20-30 mins in a bowl.

Once cooled, turn the asida out into a shallow bowl and serve with the Mulaah.

Dukwa Salat

Arugula Salad

Serves 4

3 Tomatoes, large
1 Cucumber
Rocket or Arugula leaves
1 bunch of Spring onions
2 tbsp Peanut Butter
2 tbsp Oil
Salt, to taste

Wash the arugula or rocket leaves.

Dice the tomatoes, cucumbers, and spring onions into small pieces.

Add the peanut butter, oil, salt to taste and mix all the ingredients together in a bowl until fully combined and serve.

Tip: Rinse your onions in water before
chopping, it helps to prevents crying.

Acknowledgments

We would like to express our heartfelt gratitude to everyone who contributed to the creation of this recipe book.

Special thanks to:
Our talented chefs Nastaran, Kheira, Lilli, Mahmoud, for sharing your culinary expertise and creating scrumptious dishes that have delighted our taste buds. You made every meal with love and dedication.

Our project team — Chris Niem, Eliana Nutland, and Nicholas Lo — for your creativity, diligence, and brilliant editorial coordination. Special thanks to Dave Matthews, Ralph Boer, Niwa Liwali, Hagir Ahmed, Mohammed Amin and Alec Aguilera who pioneered the community café. The tireless illustrator designer, Mieke, who brought creativity and attention to detail to every aspect of this book, ensuring it is both visually stunning and easy to follow. Thank you for capturing the vision and heart of this book and bringing it to life.

The HTB Social Transformation Leaders, Suzanne Day and Sam Coates, for facilitating this book and steering the vision of this project. Our Community Café guests, for your unwavering support, encouragement, and patience throughout the recipe testing and book production process. You were the first to taste these recipes.

Our readers and food enthusiasts, who will share love, memories, and these delicious meals with the world. Thank you all for being a part of this culinary journey. Without your support and passion for great food, this book would not have been possible.

Bon appétit!
بالهناء والشفاء
¡Buen provecho!

Milton Keynes UK
Ingram Content Group UK Ltd.
UKRC031505220724
445779UK00004B/22

* 9 7 8 1 8 3 5 3 8 2 7 1 4 *